A BRANCH
OF
BEACH PLUM

Books by Donald W. Baker

Twelve Hawks
Formal Application
Unposted Letters
The Day Before: New Poems
The Readiness: Poems From the Cape
Search Patterns
Fought By Boys: New and Selected Poems From War
A Branch of Beach Plum

A BRANCH
OF
BEACH PLUM

Donald W. Baker

Orleans, Massachusetts

Copyright © 2017 by Alison Baker

All rights reserved
Parts of this book may be
reproduced with attribution.

Some of the poems herein were first published in The Cape Codder, Eureka Literary Magazine, Interim, The Shakespeare Newsletter, Stet, and *The Worcester Review*

ISBN-13: 978-0-9978922-1-5
ISBN-10:0997892218

Cover illustration by Pamela Turnbull
Author photograph by Douglas P. Calisch

Sugar Creek Poetry Series, Volume 5
Second edition

Tickenoak Publications
Orleans, Massachusetts

For my students

CONTENTS

PROLOGUE
I, i / 3

THE ART
Beginner's Workshop: What Is Poetry? She Asked / 6
Canon / 7
Beginner's Workshop: How Do You Write a Poem? / 8
The Authorship of Shakespeare's Plays / 9
Beginner's Workshop: What Shall I Write About? / 10
Imagination / 11
Craft / 12
Poem / 13
Back / 14
The Beginning Of an End / 15

THE ARTIST
Mythology / 18
Myth / 19
Makers / 20
Splendor / 21
An Artist / 22
Dusk / 23
The Lioness / 24
Then / 25
Concerto / 26
Curtain / 27
Shock / 28
Morning / 29

THE APPLICATION
A Branch of Beach Plum / 32
Love / 33
June Song / 34
Joy / 35
Wings / 36
Longing / 37
100 Miles In Those Days Were Like 1000 Today / 38
Parting / 39
Commuting To Boston / 40
Again / 41
At the Corner Store / 42
Wish / 43

AFTER WORDS
Full of Truth We Are All Dumb / 46
Conversations We Never Had / 47
An Old One / 48

PROLOGUE

I, i

What happened in his head,
the young man from Stratford,
entering London?

Make it an April day,
he squinting in sunlight,
keeping a tight rein.

Bumpkin, hick,
spare shirt in a satchel,
looking for a house to stay in,
and The Theatre, The Curtain.

All those actors under the scalp,
yawning, beginning to dress,
and the musicians,
tuning, practicing phrases.

THE ART

BEGINNER'S WORKSHOP:
What Is Poetry? She Asked

Well, there's Poetry
with a capital P –
But there are poetries
with small p's –
as many of those
as there are tongues

billions, in fact
as plentiful as blossoms
dropping
in the orchard
and as fragrant
and as fruitful

When you bite into the apple
notice the glossy skin
the tight flesh
the harmony
of red and juice and
small brown seeds.

CANON

We do not yet have a great poem that conveys it.
I don't mean the plunge of murder
       and flash of damnation.
I mean the imperceptible crumbling of the temple steps.

BEGINNER'S WORKSHOP:
How Do You Write a Poem?

Don't try
to make literature
That stagey stuff
was done once for all
by Keats and that crowd
And flowers and birds –
if I see another
about autumn leaves
I'll –

Hunt elsewhere
like Emily D
and Doc Williams
who went in
with pen and typewriter
and came out
with an idiom
that roars like fire
even when it whispers
though we fools
take generations
to learn it

An American tongue
is sharp, noisy, irreverent
imperative as a drill press –

A song of saxifrage
A letter from Amherst.

THE AUTHORSHIP OF SHAKESPEARE'S PLAYS

A professional built these precise machines,
not some dabbler in a courtly tower.

BEGINNER'S WORKSHOP:
What Shall I Write About?

I haven't been there
and there can be no guide
but I will tell you this:
once you start to walk
its squares and alleys
or better still explore
its utility tunnels
where vein and nerve connect
you'll find you've lived there
all your life

Open your Eye then
to the tired woman
driving on the boulevard
the old man
frowning from his window
especially the sleeping lovers
behind their motel wall –
Listen: you know them all
your hand has always carried
their names and voices

Set them carefully down
how lovely
how precisely true
Now: take up your pencil
and begin

IMAGINATION

The book closed, you gaze across sand and water into some troubled distance of your own.

CRAFT

To make a poem
put a word as solid as "rung"
into every line.

Ezra told me, the chest of tools,
Denise insisted,
breath of the nervous moon.

Then the essay
will build itself
strong, straight,
a ladder through leaves.

POEMS

You must keep on removing the words, one by one.
At some point, then, you will reach an acceptable balance
between the joy with which you began to sing
and the despair that enriches the end of a failing song.

BACK

Return
to the poets of apprenticeship

Pound
the chisel
Eliot
the voice

No longer fashionable
they remain responsible

hard
as granite

pure
as a flute.

THE BEGINNING OF AN END

Walking back to the hotel in the rain,
married happily and beloved to Miss Elizabeth Bennet,
yes I said yes I will yes

THE ARTIST

MYTHOLOGY

We need those tales,
that they,
not we,
are the bad ones,

that the crushed limbs
and broken hearts
are their debris.

The clear mind
and the pure soul
are, of course, ours,

we who are well-saved,
who, like vampires,
avoid mirrors.

MYTH

Supine on the sand, your body drenched in sunlight,
suppose you took fire, suppose you became a sacred flame
and blazed, blinding and untouchable,
through the rest of my life.

MAKERS

I told him –
I said, Dammit
you stay close
you watch me

But that kid –
they know it all
don't they?

When he started up
I yelled
For God's sake
stay low!

He was strong
agile
mounted like a hawk
a speck out of earshot.

And the sun –
that bastard Apollo
up there
grinning.

And just as I said
the wax ran
he splashed
and I –
I came on home.

SPLENDOR

The stubborn bravery of the human heart
that beats its way through folly, malice, and duplicity
towards an undiscoverable shore.

AN ARTIST

A man stood at the top of a bluff,
looking down at the sea, where it hawked
and spat again and again on the land.

You, sea, are my model, he said.
I admire your nonchalance and disdain.
If I had your years I too could be perfect.

And the man looked deep into time
where the rivers swelled
and the land cowered before the waters.

O loitering sea, said the man,
when you come into your property,
you and your gangs of rain,

and the mountains are yours,
and the valleys with all their bones,
and all the jewels of the cities,

remember the eyes that made you,
the tongue that gave you a name.
And he returned to his trade.

The sea shrugged, flashing its teeth,
and, with a flick of a finger,
removed a wrinkle of sand.

DUSK

Wandering among the white, twisted oaks, I came upon
that lichened slab of granite, stubbornly erect,
set for Captain Esau Baker, lost to the Atlantic long ago.

THE LIONESS

A man said to his neighbors,
the sea is coming,
the tide is already climbing the dunes.

Yet the sun shone in its cloudless way,
and the sea, with a heavy sigh,
stretched like a lioness in her dream.

Nevertheless, the man muttered,
I know a sign when I sense one.
And he collected his portables.

That night, while his neighbors forgot
and embraced in their beds,
the man lay and listened:

the sea gathered its gales,
and roared, and tore at the land
in a tempest, and the land shook.

At sunrise the sea lay purring,
its wavelets, playful as cubs,
worrying conch shells and pebbles.

Nevertheless, repeated the man,
nevertheless.
And he pulled his blanket over his head.

THEN

We talked at the edge of the cliff, the surf hammering below,
then walked in silence back across the moor.
How would I answer now, hearing those bitter words?

CONCERTO

The violinist –
              arms bending
    to her instrument

black hair
        eyes cast down
                lips parted –

    trembling
to the gradual passion
              Of the strings.

For whom?
              The mind drops
      from her green

            vivace
into shadowy
    largo –

how subtle
            the luxury
    of the box

    the lush vibrato –
how flushed
            the fondled notes.

CURTAIN

No dialogue, only music, a flutesong, diminuendo.
And the old man in a splash of lamplight,
bent to his desk, writing.

SHOCK

The meter-reader
steps down
from her pickup truck
kicks across the leaves

With stubby pencil
enters
carefully
the numbers

claps
the notebook shut
strolls back
whistling

Caught as she lifts
one foot
to mount her cab
squints across her shoulder

The sun
through lattice
of branches
falls upon her

glories in her hair
ravishes her mouth
with quick hot
hunger

MORNING

I never told you how at last the sunrise burst into the room,
how I strolled to the restaurant on the dock,
sat alone above the harbor wash, sipping coffee,
retrieving life.

THE APPLICATION

A BRANCH OF BEACH PLUM

Most days I walk the old track under the pines
and over the dunes to the beach.
I have chosen for you the bend in the path
where a thicket of beach plum survives the backhoes,
where at noon in our season the air
used to be heavy with the smell of blossoms.
This morning I walked on the brown needles
as gently as I could so that no abrupt
gesture would temper the music of the warblers
in the spruce. Returning, I broke off
a branch of beach plum and carried it home.
Now it rises from the blue vase on the mantel,
the flowers, fragile and pink, beginning to wither,
one broken twig oozing a clear drop.
Yes, that is where I should like to meet you,
halfway between home and the shore, knowing
that back there are kitchen and books and bedroom,
a house full of lives and living,
and, not far ahead, the comforting sea.

LOVE

Nothing can render it,
not the rose, nor the summer's day, nor the
          bracelet of bright hair,
Yet through the nuclear brain the stubborn heart beats,
     as best it can, its noises into music.

JUNE SONG

The wren
from Carolina
smallest
on our block

shrieks somewhere
up there
against that blue
above that pine

teakettle teakettle
teakettle
is aboil
ready

ready ready
to drink to
this morning
this June

this summer
or this dewy
anything
you care

to drink to –
oh tiny
bird oh giant
exultation!

JOY

On our way home the blue balloon escaped
my daughter's hand, and climbed,
trailing her giggle, towards the brilliant clouds.

WINGS

We spoke of the games of our childhood,
Kick-the-Can, Hide-and-Go-Seek,
recalled some names, had forgotten others,
the kid with buck teeth, the redhead who moved away.
The evening was calm, the wine had absolved much
of the trespass of our hearts, and our syllables slipped
cheerfully from the patio into the shadows under the pines.
Then a pair of black wings, too swift to identify,
perhaps a small owl, swooped through the dusk,
and the air was stirred. "Heavens," you murmured.
And a qualm came to me, that you and I had always played
the old games, that even now we were dodging and hiding
like those vanished children, who in fact had not vanished
but only hidden around the corner of the house
behind the lilacs, whispering and giggling, to wait
through all our years for the end of the search.
It grew darker. We sat side by side in silence,
as if listening, half-fearful, half-hopeful, for a swoop of wings.
And the stars brightened, a breeze ruffled the pines,
and that hour became with its shadowy truth
indistinguishable from the rest of the past.

LONGING

I want you not in that hour of violent pleasure,
but when your naked eyes turned to me as if startled,
seeing me for the first time as something other,
something more.

100 MILES IN THOSE DAYS WERE LIKE 1000 TODAY

The Model-A
rattled
up the hills
backfired
down the vales
Dad at the wheel
erect and whistling
his blue eyes
fastened
on some fantastic
future
that still eludes us all.

PARTING

An elm tree, a dusty street, Ford turning the corner:
how easy it was, and no one to prophesy that fifty years on
mere words would become magic symbols and music.

COMMUTING TO BOSTON

Driving alone, you sing whatever you like:
La ci darem, Sentimental Journey.
Tears fill people's eyes.

You make a speech against war.
The President, a spokesman informs you,
is deeply impressed.

Near Weymouth, you enter *King Lear*:
"...from the depths of an intense despair,
the contemplation of the infinite."
A whole theater is moved to silence.

Back in the kitchen, no doubt,
your wife, sipping coffee,
flips the pages of *The New Yorker*.

Yes, that is indeed who you are:
preaching the liberal mind,
dreaming of luxury.

That, in fact, is the point you've been trying to make,
the self-deceit, the indulgence,
the adolescent ideals...

Look. The harbor. Towers and fog.
A blonde in a blue Mercedes.
Tonight, after the rush hour,
move the guns.
Emplace them on Dorchester Heights.
You could, like Washington,
take the city.

AGAIN

I imagine you along the highway, into the city,
up the familiar stair,
while here, in sunlight on the dunes,
nothing seems broken.
My watch, for instance, continues to tick
with a perfect integrity.

AT THE CORNER STORE

The old man
totters now and then
plodding
towards the store

life holding on
to buy
bread and orange juice
for breakfast

out of the shadows
blinking
in the early
sunlight –

he resembles another
younger
long ago
but the same blue eyes.

WISH

I shall knock, and enter a room full of books.
A small woman in white and a doctor from New Jersey
will pause in their conversation to nod to a newcomer.

AFTER WORDS

FULL OF TRUTH WE ARE ALL DUMB

All my life I tried to speak the language
that knocked against my tongue
whenever I wept or prayed or kissed.
In a rage to touch that other heart,
envying the eloquent commanders,
I failed in bitter ignorance of idiom.
Now good phrases crowd into my mind
like a choir gathering for service.
Words are singing: *truth, courage, love*;
the syntax bears its holy burden:
vindication, a memorial
for the voiceless boy, the stammering man.
But the ear I would propitiate is dust,
the shoulder I would stand to long since ashes.

CONVERSATIONS WE NEVER HAD

Conversations we never had come to life in me now.
We are eloquent, full of pictures and song.
Like artists we work our way back
                toward the consummate silence.

AN OLD ONE

The old poet's music chuckles from the page,
childlike rhythms, compassionate chords,
melody on the edge of wisdom.
It seems clear that he has almost perfected his song.

www.ingramcontent.com/pod-product-compliance
Lightning Source LLC
Chambersburg PA
CBHW022125040426
42450CB00006B/851